FRUIT OF THE SPIRIT

FAITHFULNESS

Fruit of the Spirit Study Guide Series

Love

Joy

Peace

Patience

Kindness

Goodness

Faithfulness

Gentleness

Self-Control

CALVIN MILLER

FRUIT OF THE SPIRIT

FAITHFULNESS

Published in Nashville, Tennessee, by Thomas Nelson. Thomas Nelson is a trademark of Thomas Nelson, Inc.

Thomas Nelson, Inc., titles may be purchased in bulk for educational, business, fund-raising, or sales promotional use. For information, please e-mail SpecialMarkets@ThomasNelson.com.

Typesetting by Gregory C. Benoit Publishing, Old Mystic, CT GᴄᴮB

ISBN: 978-1-4185-2842-3

Printed in the United States of America
08 09 10 11 12 RRD 9 8 7 6 5 4 3 2 1

TABLE OF CONTENTS

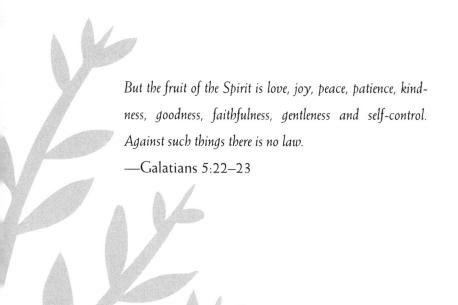

But the fruit of the Spirit is love, joy, peace, patience, kindness, goodness, faithfulness, gentleness and self-control. Against such things there is no law.

—Galatians 5:22–23

INTRODUCTION

Society tells us that faithfulness is an archaic concept; the Bible tells us faithfulness is who God is. One idea is right, the other is wrong. In the Old Testament, God established covenants that were guaranteed by his character. When the prophets of Baal faced off against Elijah, God's faithfulness came through. Time and time again, God showed that he keeps his promises; he is faithful.

That characteristic is realized in the lives of believers only as we allow God to dominate our lives. By nature we are promise breakers; God is the promise keeper. If we desire to be promise keepers, we must first allow God's character to override our character. It's the ultimate makeover.

If God had ever broken one of his promises, we would have reason to never trust him. Yet he shows us perfect faithfulness. We, on the other hand, probably have more examples of faithlessness than we'd care to admit.

God's promises never sleep. They are the heartbeat of nature resounding in the pulse of our existence. The promise of a Savior came alive in that Bethlehem manger. The promise of redemption accompanied Golgotha's cross. The promise of eternity rose on that resurrection Sunday. In our minds, promises were made to be broken; in God's mind, promises are made to be kept.

That's where this study comes in. This isn't about learning to be faithful; it's about letting God's faithfulness become the essence of who you are. It's not about getting something; it's about becoming something. You can never be faithful until you allow God to become your faithfulness. Therefore, this study will move you toward a relationship with God that invites his faithfulness to become yours.

HOW TO USE THIS GUIDE

Galatians 5:22–23 is not a plan to achieve better faith. Rather, it is a description of God's personal gifts to all of us. If we follow God and seek his blessing, then the fruits of the Spirit are a natural overflow in our relationship with God. We are to grow in character so that one day we will reflect the image of our Lord.

This series of nine six-week studies will clearly focus your spiritual life to become more like Christ. Each study guide is divided into six weeks, and each of the six-week courses covers one of the fruits of the Spirit. Participants simply read each daily study and answer the questions at the end of each devotional. This prepares everyone for the group discussion at the end of the week.

Each week features a similar pattern that explores one aspect of that study's fruit of the Spirit. The first lesson establishes the aspect of the fruit to be explored throughout the week. The second lesson looks at the week's theme as it relates to God's purpose in the life of the believer. The third lesson looks at the week's theme as it relates to the believer's relationship with Christ. The fourth lesson explores how the fruit is relevant in service to others. And in the fifth lesson, the theme is related to personal worship. A sixth lesson is included as a bonus study, and focuses on either a biblical character who modeled this particular fruit, or a key parable that brings the theme into focus.

Each weeklong study should conclude in a group review. The weekly group discussion serves as a place to understand the practical side of the theme and receive encouragement and feedback on the journey to become more Christlike. For the study to have the character-transforming effect God desires, it is important for the participant to spend ten to twenty minutes a day reading the Scripture passage and the devotional, and to think through the two questions for the day. If each participant reads all of the questions beforehand, it greatly enhances the group dynamic. Each participant should choose three or four questions to discuss during the group session.

These simple guidelines will help make group time productive. Take a total of about forty-five minutes to answer and discuss the questions. Each person need not answer every question, but be sure all members participate. You can stimulate participation by having everyone respond to an icebreaker question. Have each group member answer the first of the six questions listed at the end of the week, and leave the remaining questions open-ended. Or, make up your own icebreaker question, such as: What color best represents the day you are having? What is your favorite movie? Or, how old were you when you had your first kiss?

No one should respond to all of the questions. Keep in mind that if you are always talking, the others are not. It is essential that everyone contribute. If you notice that someone is not participating, ask that group member which question is the most relevant. Be sensitive if something is keeping that member from contributing. Don't ask someone to read or pray aloud unless you know that the member is comfortable with such a task.

Always start and end your time with prayer. Sometimes it helps to have each person say what he or she plans to do with the lesson that week. Remember to reserve ten minutes for group prayer. You might want to keep a list of requests and answers to prayer at the back of this book.

Week 1: God's Blessing on Faithfulness

Memory Passage for the Week: Revelation 2:10b

Day 1: God's Blessing on Faithfulness

God longs to bless us. He is faithful to us. When we are faithful to him, blessings abound. Genesis 12:1–4a.

Day 2: The Purpose of God in My Life

Faithfulness is a gift anyone can give God. And when his purposes for our lives are fulfilled, we are blessed beyond our expectations. Deuteronomy 10:20–22.

Day 3: My Relationship with Christ

The blessing attached to faithfulness is the blessing of eternal salvation. No blessing could be a greater reward. Matthew 24:9–13.

Day 4: My Service to Others

Faithfulness is not just a gift of the Spirit; it is a worldview—the basis of our eternal rewards according to this passage. Matthew 25:31–40.

Day 5: My Personal Worship

Surely heaven must pay special attention to those worshipers who are persistent and faithful in praising God. Hebrews 11:8–12.

Day 6: A Character Study on Abraham

Genesis 15:1–6; 22:1–18

Day 7: Group Discussion

Day 1: God's Blessing on Faithfulness

Read Genesis 12:1—4a

We don't know much about Abram and Sarai when God called them to originate the Jewish nation. We only know they were old and that they came from Ur, a pagan society. Many suggest that they were moon worshipers serving celestial gods and goddesses.

Then suddenly a previously unheard voice broke into their world. It was the voice of a God much mightier than the gods they worshiped—it was "the" God. This unknown God spoke to them and said, "Leave your country, your people and your father's household and go to the land that I will show you" (Genesis 12:1). And with this brief summons, Abram and Sarai, old in years—some would say too old to make such a pilgrimage—had the audacity to obey God.

Judaism was born in this simple way. At the time, few people recognized the significance of Abram and Sarai's trip. Yet this is the way God works. He often alters history by starting with the smallest instructions. A baby in a stable or an old couple doddering out of the moon temples of the Tigris valley are just two examples of God's unique methodology.

In such ordinary things comes the roar of God. The quaking world is reborn in the name of people who obey the extraordinary claim God holds on their lives. In their faithfulness, God's blessings swallow them whole.

Have you ever heard a simple, seemingly unimportant whisper? Did it fail to make perfect sense? Listen! God waits to bless you. He longs to bless you. All you have to do is say, "Yes, Lord, I will!" Then act. Open your heart and follow with faithfulness. Be obedient in simple matters and the angels will come to attention.

Questions for Personal Reflection

1. Have you ever felt that you were hearing a whisper from God? What did he say to you?

2. When hearing what you believe to be God, how do you know for sure it is God? What keeps you from acting in faith in response to God's calling?

Day 2: The Purpose of God in My Life
Read Deuteronomy 10:20–22

Moses reminded the Israelites that God took them into Egypt as a group of only seventy souls. Four hundred years later, Israel emerged as a nation. It is not uncommon for God's promises to not be completely fulfilled in our lifetime. God made the promise of nationhood to Abram and Sarai in Genesis 12, and even at the end of Abraham's life, Israel was still only a very small nation of three. But in a day long after his death, the nation numbered in the millions.

Faithfulness always serves God's purposes, but often the mills of God grind slowly. Many times we only see God's enduring intentions in hindsight. Even as Abraham died, he could not measure the extent of the promise that grew from his faithfulness. That finished vision was perhaps a score of lifetimes away. Still the promises of God never sleep.

Faithfulness instructs us how to live with purpose, but even better, we can pass it to our children until—as Abraham discovered—the world is blessed because of that simple discipline called obedience.

Faithfulness is a gift anyone can give God, and he responds with a purpose for every morning's sunrise. Then at last we are free. We live and have great reasons to live.

Questions for Personal Reflection

1. Faith is passed from generation to generation. What has been your life teaching about God?

2. Faithfulness produces obedience. What are some things you can do to nurture faithfulness in your life?

Day 3: My Relationship with Christ

Read Matthew 24:9–13

We Christians in the West have gotten used to cheap grace. To be a Christian is often to become a part of a prosperous, comfortable, and safe community. Our church attendance hardly suffers a threat. But in this passage Jesus taught that we should be openly faithful even when our witness puts us in danger. Jesus was about to become a martyr himself; he knew his faith would require his own life, and this was also a possibility for all followers. So he called us to be faithful even when our faithfulness will be very costly:

> *When we are to be handed over to be persecuted and put to death ... (Matthew 24:9).*
> *When we are hated by all people in all nations ... (v. 9).*
> *When all people fall away from the faith and betray and hate each other ... (v. 10).*
> *When many false prophets appear and deceive many ... (v. 11).*

In all of these circumstances we are to be faithful in our relationship with Christ. But notice the reward: "He who stands firm to the end will be saved" (v. 13). Here Jesus used the usual New Testament word for "saved," but not in reference to the normal state of salvation. This is salvation with a capitol "s." It is that state of final being, face to face with Christ for eternity.

The word *saved* sometimes refers to initially meeting Christ. *Saved* sometimes indicates an ongoing relationship with Christ. But this use refers to that unending union when we, who have longed to see him without even a cloud between us, are at last standing in Jesus' presence forever. This salvation indeed is the plum of our faithfulness to be picked from the tree of our obedience.

Questions for Personal Reflection

1. How is your salvation affecting the way you live your daily life?

2. If you died today, where would you spend eternity? How do you know?

Day 4: My Service to Others

Read Matthew 25:31–40

At first glance, this passage in the book of Matthew appears to conflict with grace. Jesus discussed how faith in practice compels us to serve others. Grace is God's free gift—no strings attached. But grace should call forth from us one grand response: service! You can't earn salvation, but the parable suggests that those who know they are heaven-bound should be so delighted that they reply with obedient living.

There was a sweet naiveté among the disciples. They seemed surprised at this wholehearted and overwhelming commendation. "When did we see you hungry and feed you, or thirsty and give you something to drink? When did we see you a stranger and invite you in, or needing clothes and clothe you? When did we see you sick or in prison and go to visit you?" (Matthew 25:37–39).

Jesus made it clear: ministry to any human needs writes the name of Jesus on the very forehead of the person we help.

Being in Calcutta at the time of Mother Teresa's death, I was among those westerners allowed to visit as she lay in state. I will never forget seeing her bare feet protrude from underneath the flag of India. Seeing the calloused feet of this tiny woman reminded me that for years she walked the ghettos of a dismal place and managed to turn some of Calcutta into a "city of joy." I remember she taught that when anyone attended a dying parishioner, he attended the body of Christ himself.

When we meet anyone vile and diseased, we shouldn't think, *Poor thing—how horrible.* We must think, *Jesus, I see you. I will help because you gave me a future in you, and in the meantime, no one will endure this human hell without my ministry.*

Questions for Personal Reflection

1. What is your first response when you encounter someone in need?

2. What should be your reaction to the needy you encounter?

Day 5: My Personal Worship

Read Hebrews 11:8–12

Here the New Testament recorded Abraham's final celebration of God's reward for his faithfulness. How do sincere believers react when overwhelmed by God's faithfulness? They worship.

Abraham's greatness wasn't born from celebrating God only once his dreams came true. Abraham was great because he celebrated God before he saw those dreams fulfilled. Abraham first received God's promise in Genesis 12. Time is quite compact in this passage—a scant five verses later he entered the land, and, "He built an altar there to the LORD, who had appeared to him" (v. 7).

Abraham built this altar at Bethel, which means "house of the Lord." These words suggest that the altar would be a place to return to again and again as he trusted God's faithfulness. It isn't hard to worship God for the promises he has already fulfilled. It is a mark of real faith to worship while we *wait* for God's promises. Hebrews 11 says Abraham worshiped while he looked for a "city with foundations, whose architect and builder is God" (v. 10).

Have you learned the art of worshiping the Christ who has promised he will come? It hasn't happened yet, but be faithful and worship him. Somewhere in time, all will be done exactly as he has said. He is the promise keeper. He saved you to worship him with no cloud against your confidence in his promises.

Sing to your Lord each morning, "Jesus, if I do not see your promises fulfilled today, I will praise you while I wait for tomorrow."

Questions for Personal Reflection

1. Is your faith response to God proactive in that you trust God before He does something? Why or why not?

2. How should the promises of God affect the way you live today?

Day 6: Abraham—Unwavering Fidelity

Read Genesis 15:1–6; 22:1–18

Faithfulness trusts when the final form of our circumstances cannot be seen. God promised Abraham that he would father a great nation. But Abraham was an old man whose wife was well past her childbearing years. The child God promised was to be born far from the land Abraham called home. Faithfulness meant Abraham was confident that all God promised would occur, even when his age and circumstances made it look impossible.

Hebrews 11:8–19 lists nine qualities of Abraham's life of faithfulness:

1. He followed God even though he did not know where God was leading (v. 8). Faith follows God through the mists of uncertain circumstances.
2. He lived in tents as a foreigner (v. 9). Being a foreigner is hard work, for it seeks a home among the unfamiliar.
3. He was looking for a city (v. 10), a kingdom that would rise silhouetted against an unborn horizon. Little did he know that the city would be called Zion, and his own children would build it in the generations to come. God's greatest dreams are only owned by those who can see beyond the frail years of their lifetime.

4. He counted on God's promise that even as an old man he would become a father (v. 11).

5. Abraham considered God faithful (v. 11), one who did not make idle promises.

6. Abraham saw that God would be faithful in time beyond his own (v. 13). All that God said would come to pass.

7. Abraham longed for the coming of a wonderful kingdom (v. 16). Good people of faith believe that wonder—the glorious wonder of God—is on the way.

8. Abraham was so faithful that he did not refuse to give God his only beloved son when God asked him for the most precious thing in his life (v. 17). In this matter of faithfulness, Abraham approached the faithfulness of God who gave his only begotten Son to redeem the world.

9. Abraham's faith was so great that he knew that even if he killed his own son at God's request, God could raise him from the dead (v. 19). Faithfulness always sees that nothing is impossible for God.

Abraham remains the Bible's epitome of faithfulness, and from such faithfulness the Hebrew nation came to be.

Questions for Personal Reflection

1. How does your faithfulness to God compare to that of Abraham?

2. What might happen in your life if you trusted God the way Abraham trusted

him?

Day 7: Group Discussion

The following questions should take about forty-five minutes to answer and discuss. Each member should answer the first question, leaving the remaining questions open-ended. Everyone need not answer, but be sure all members participate.

1. *Which of God's promises are most meaningful or comforting to you?*

2. *What are some of the ways God speaks to us?*

3. *In what areas of life do we need to be more faithful to God?*

4. *How is salvation a past, present, and future event?*

5. How can you become a person who puts faith into action?

6. What seemingly impossible situation do you trust God to overcome? What is the nature of your prayer regarding this matter?

Week 2: Faithfulness—The High Art of Persistence
Memory Passage for the Week: 1 Thessalonians 5:16–18

Day 1: Faithfulness—The High Art of Persistence
When prayerful persistence is inspired by our desperation to hear from heaven, angels bless our faithfulness. Luke 18:1–8.

Day 2: The Purpose of God in My Life
Faithfulness means seeking God until you find him, knocking until he opens. 2 Chronicles 27:1–6.

Day 3: My Relationship with Christ
Job made persistence such a priority that not even death would end his constant struggle to be with God. So should we pursue Christ, until the union we seek from him is ours for eternity. Job 13:15.

Day 4: My Service to Others
Nothing is more beautiful than the prayer warrior who is persistent on behalf of someone else's need. Luke 11:5–8.

Day 5: My Personal Worship
Faithfulness isn't satisfied until it sees—at close range—the God it cannot quit dreaming about. There in God's nearness great worship is born. Psalm 15:1–4.

Day 6: A Character Study on Elijah
1 Kings 18:16–39

Day 7: Group Discussion

Day 1: Faithfulness—The High Art of Persistence

Read Luke 18:1–8

One of the prayer outlines many are taught to use when they first learn to pray consists of four parts:

Adoration

Contrition

Thanksgiving

Supplication

But in the parable of Luke 18:1–8, it seems Jesus would have added the word *persistence* to that prayer outline. It doesn't fit the ACTS acrostic, but persistence indicates we're serious about the work of prayer.

Persistence in the act of prayer is not verbiage—extra words don't prayers more brilliant or powerful. Persistence is intentional. It is desire. It wants from God. It hungers for God. It will not rest.

Jesus told a parable about a poor widow who persistently pestered a judge. Her desperation made her return again and again to the only one who could help her, and she would not cease. The judge, like God, honored her persistence. God answers those whose agendas will not quit, whose needs will not stop turning to him for fulfillment.

When prayerful persistence is inspired by our desperation to hear from heaven, angels bless our faithfulness.

Questions for Personal Reflection

1. What is one area of life or one issue about which you need to hear from God?

2. Is there anything keeping you from praying persistently? Explain.

Day 2: The Purpose of God in My Life
Read 2 Chronicles 27:1–6

Jotham grew powerful because he walked steadfastly with the Lord his God. Jotham was persistent, and his nonstop faithfulness bought him to Judah's throne with a powerful influence. We tend to find God's purpose for us when we pursue his will for us with persistence.

It is what we are not told about Jotham that most fascinates me. What had happened in Jotham's life to break his spirit and teach him persistent dependency on God? It can hardly be doubted that somewhere in the unrecorded years of his life, he learned the lessons of brokenness, dependency, and trust.

Broken pride is a beautiful gift we lay on the highest level of God's altars. The gift comes wrapped in our bandages and slings or in our handkerchief once soaked with our tears.

Gene Edwards wrote so beautifully in *A Tale of Three Kings*:

> God has a university. It's a small school. Few enroll, even fewer graduate—very few indeed. God has this school because he does not have broken men. Instead he has several other types of men. He has men who claim to be God's authority ... and aren't; men who claim to be broken and aren't.... He has, regretfully, a spectroscopic mixture of everything in between. All of these he has in abundance; but broken men, hardly at all.[1]

There is an important relationship between brokenness and persistence. Jotham found that relationship and found his purpose in the world. When we grow mature enough to embrace our brokenness, we find our purpose in life.

Questions for Personal Reflection

1. Describe the last time you expressed your brokenness to God.

2. How did your expression of brokenness affect your relationship with God?

Day 3: My Relationship with Christ
Read Job 13:15

"Though he slay me, yet will I hope in him," cried Job (Job 13:15). Job made a decision to stick with God. He pointed out that life hadn't treated him very well, but he was not about to give up his relationship with God.

Why was Job so dogmatic? Could it be that our faithfulness is an inevitable response to God's faithfulness? Jeremiah wrote in Lamentations 3:19–24:

> *I remember my affliction and my wandering,*
> *   the bitterness and the gall.*
> *I well remember them,*
> *   and my soul is downcast within me.*
> *Yet this I call to mind*
> *   and therefore I have hope:*
> *Because of the LORD's great love we are not consumed,*
> *   for his compassions never fail.*
> *They are new every morning;*
> *   great is your faithfulness.*
> *I say to myself, "The LORD is my portion;*
> *   therefore I will wait for him."*

There you have it. Jeremiah, like Job, understood that all we have needed God's hand has provided.

Faithfulness makes a habit of hanging around God. Living close to God doesn't necessarily equal less suffering (Job is proof). However, it does mean that in the clear light of our nearness to God, we can better see what suffering means—and what our faithfulness should produce.

God has been faithful. He will be faithful. Jesus, his Son, was faithful to the point of death, and our relationship is guaranteed by the covenant of Calvary.

Questions for Personal Reflection

1. How would you describe your closeness to God?

2. How does it feel when you are close to God? How does it feel when you are not as close to him?

Day 4: My Service to Others

Read Luke 11:5–8

This parable illustrates the high art of persistence and its efficacy in prayer. Praying faithfully means we are willing to go boldly before the throne and ask what we want from God again and again.

Notice the persistence in this paraphrase of Jesus' parable:

The Requisitioner: Friend, let me have three loaves of bread. I've had a friend drop in—a hungry friend who eats like a horse.

The Groggy Neighbor: Good grief! Do you have any idea what time it is? My kids are in bed, my door is bolted. What do you think I am—an all-night bakery?

The Requisitioner: Pretty please?

The Groggy Neighbor: No, be reasonable.

The Requisitioner: I'm gonna knock and knock on your door; may I please have some bread?

The Groggy Neighbor: Oh, all right, come on over. I'll give you the bread and then maybe we'll both get a little sleep.

It may come as a surprise that Jesus commended the neighbor for acting boldly and persistently until he got what he needed.

Boldness is the key in faithful petitioning. The same is true in our service to those around us. Service almost always calls for persistence.

Bringing the message of God's love to the world requires bold, persistent prayer on the part of the messenger. God told us to boldly claim the desires and needs of our hearts.

Questions for Personal Reflection

1. What are your most desperate needs?

2. What is the value of persistently seeking God when it comes to your needs?

Day 5: My Personal Worship
Read Psalm 15:1–4

"Who may dwell in your sanctuary?" asked the psalmist (Psalm 15:1). He then answered his own question by saying, "[He] who keeps his oath even when it hurts" (v. 4). Belief without faithfulness amounts to nothing. Furthermore, faithfulness inspires a hunger to have not just the things of God, but God himself. Faithfulness isn't satisfied until it sees—at close range—the God it cannot quit dreaming about. There in God's nearness great worship is born.

This is the grand distinction between true Christianity and one of many counterfeits. True Christianity hungers not for God's blessings, but for the presence of God himself.

Thomas á Kempis perfectly expressed the heart of faithfulness when he wrote:

> *Grant me, O most loving Lord, to rest in thee above all creatures, above all health and beauty, above all glory and honor, above all power and dignity, above all knowledge and subtlety, above all riches and art, above all fame and praise, above all sweetness and comfort, above all hope and promise, above all gifts and favors that thou canst give and impart to us, and above all jubilee that the mind of man can receive and feel; finally above all angels and archangels, and above*

all heavenly hosts, and above all things visible and invisible, and above all that thou art not, O my God. It is too small and unsatisfying, whatever thou bestowest on me apart from thee, or revealed to me or promised, whilst thou are not seen, and not fully obtained. For surely my heart cannot truly rest or be entirely contented, unless it rest in thee. [2]

Questions for Personal Reflection

1. In what ways are you craving God's presence in your life?

2. How should your desire for God affect the way you worship?

Day 6: Elijah—Taking a Stand, Even when You Are Alone

Read 1 Kings 18:16–39

The contest on Mt. Carmel was definitely a faith-crisis in Israel's history. It seemed to Elijah that if things got any worse, evil would win. So he threw out his challenge to Israel's wicked king: "You have abandoned the LORD's commands and have followed the Baals. Now summon the people from all over Israel to meet me on Mt. Carmel. And bring the four hundred and fifty prophets of Baal and the four hundred prophets of Asherah, who eat at Jezebel's table" (1 Kings 18:18–19). The word went out, and hosts of innumerable pagans met with the sole prophet of the living God. Mt. Carmel was thronged by hundreds of pilgrims eager to see what the day would bring. Elijah challenged them:

> *How long will you waver between two opinions? If the LORD is God, follow him; but if Baal is God, follow him.... I am the only one of the LORD's prophets left, but Baal has four hundred and fifty prophets. Get two bulls for us. Let them choose one for themselves, and let them cut it into pieces and put it on the wood but not set fire to it. I will prepare the other bull and put it on the wood but not set fire to it. Then you call on the name of your god, and I will call on the name of the LORD. The god who answers by fire—he is God.*
> —vv. 21–24

The contest began.

Does faithfulness matter?

Is it a virtue that ends in triumph?

Consider the reward of those who boldly stand alone: "Then the fire of the LORD fell ... the people saw this, they fell prostrate and cried, 'The LORD—he is God! The LORD, he is God!'" (vv. 38–39).

To know you're right is to understand that God's smile is more important than others' approval. If Elijah waited for a national consensus, he would never have gone to Mt. Carmel. The right time to take a stand is when the only position thinking people will tolerate is the wrong one. Right is rarely established by popular vote.

The faithful must often stand while the masses stay seated. The faithful are not those who treasure popularity, but those who continually wonder how God sees them.

Questions for Personal Reflection

1. Are you more concerned with becoming like the world or becoming like God?

2. What are some areas of your life in which you desire to become more like

God?

Day 7: Group Discussion

The following questions should take about forty-five minutes to answer and discuss. Each member should answer the first question, leaving the remaining questions open-ended. Everyone need not answer, but be sure all members participate.

1.   *What are some concerns that warrant praying persistently?*

2.   *How has God responded to your persistent prayers?*

3.   *What lessons can be learned through times of brokenness, dependency, and trust?*

4.   *What are some things we can do in order to "hang around" God? How can this affect our spiritual lives?*

5. What is the difference between craving the things of God and craving God?

6. Why do people seek to please themselves and others rather than pleasing God?

Week 3: Faithfulness—The Habit of Spiritual Dependency

Memory Passage for the Week: Proverbs 3:5–6

Day 1: Faithfulness—The Habit of Spiritual Dependency

We need God. His power is essential for conquering our personal weaknesses. Joshua 14:13–14.

Day 2: The Purpose of God in My Life

Unfailing respect causes our unrighteous souls to melt into the heart of God's holiness. With such respect we learn his wisdom. Isaiah 33:6.

Day 3: My Relationship with Christ

God will never leave us or forsake us. Our relationship with Christ is constant—not because we're constant, but because he is constant. Hebrews 13:5–9.

Day 4: My Service to Others

Moses was a faithful servant, and when the times were heavy, God was most available to stand under the yoke with him. Numbers 11:10–15.

Day 5: My Personal Worship

Worship only when it's the "thing to do," and God may not attend you, but worship when your very life is under threat, and you may be sure of his presence. Revelation 2:10.

Day 6: A Character Study on Jeremiah

Jeremiah 20:1–12

Day 7: Group Discussion

Day 1: Faithfulness—The Habit of Spiritual Dependency

Read Joshua 14:13–14

Spiritual dependency is the best habit. "Trust in the LORD with all your heart," said the writer of Proverbs. "In all your ways acknowledge him, and he will make your paths straight" (Proverbs 3:5–6).

Joshua blessed Caleb with the city of Hebron because Caleb served the Lord wholeheartedly. Caleb was one of those inheritors of promise who trusted God with his life. In Scripture, he always appeared with a positive spirit toward the plan of God in his life. In short, his very name stands for faithfulness.

Faithfulness simply means God can count on us. He can count on us to be positive when others are negative. He can count on us to obey when others are disobedient. He can count on us to follow when others bail out because of the steepness of the ascent. Faithfulness is the quality that honors God with obedience—joyful obedience. A faithfulness that grumbles at God's requirements is not faithfulness at all. It is only grudging acquiescence. Faithfulness comes from following God. God's will makes even our personal Calvarys sweet, because we are going where God leads. Sure, the nails always hurt, but the joy of standing true surpasses the pain.

Faithfulness is the habit of spiritual dependency. Caleb did not follow God so he could offer a proud example to the quitters. Caleb followed because he needed God. He was dependent on God to exhibit steadfast love and providence. Those who grow dependent on God find his power essential for conquering human weakness; "God is their refuge and strength"; he is their "ever-present help in trouble" (Psalm 46:1). They are so dependent on God that faithfulness naturally follows.

Questions for Personal Reflection

1. What are your needs, and how can your dependence on God to meet those needs yield faithfulness?

2. How do you feel when someone lets you down? How do you think God feels when you let him down?

Day 2: The Purpose of God in My Life
Read Isaiah 33:6

The best friend that our spiritual dependency has is the fear of the Lord, said Isaiah. What power there is in the reverence we give God. This awe releases us to be more than we are. All fear is outlawed for the believer except the fear of the Lord. The only trembling permitted is the terror of standing face to face with utter holiness. The people who tremble before God cannot forget the immensity of him to whom their lives are owed. We aren't just called to fear his size and power, but to tremble lest we drop the task he put us here to accomplish. It is the strength to be real in a plastic world.

In his book *The Fear of God*, Frederick Faber understood Isaiah and agreed with him:

> *Thy goodness to thy saints of old, An awful thing appeared;*
> *For were thy majesty less good, much less would it be feared.*

> *A special joy is in all love, for objects we revere;*
> *Thus joy in God will always be proportioned to our fear.*

> *When most I fear thee, Lord! Then most familiar I appear,*
> *And I am in my soul most free, When I am most in fear.*

They love thee little, if at all, Who do not fear thee much:
If love is thine attraction, Lord! Fear is thy very touch.

We fear because thou art so good, Also because we sin;
And when we make most show of love, We tremble most within.[3]

It is when we tremble most within that we understand the sufficiency of Christ and rejoice in our own need. It is in this fear we find that our faithfulness is truly the habit of spiritual dependency.

Questions for Personal Reflection

1. What does it mean to fear the Lord, and how is that fear beneficial to your spiritual life?

2. What effect does the fear of the Lord have on the other fears you face?

Day 3: My Relationship with Christ

Read Hebrews 13:5–9

God's Word never soars higher in its defense of Christ than in the book of Hebrews. Hebrews has a kind of built-in weeping conscience for the martyrs. People all around the writer of this noble letter were dying for their faith. The writer's tears spilled out in some of the most elegant writing of the New Testament. Jesus never looked better in this great book than in the thirteenth chapter. Verse 5 is the promise of glory: "Never will I leave you." Verse 8 defines his role in the life of the believer: "Jesus Christ is the same yesterday and today and forever."

He never abandons us—ever! What comfort this must have been to the martyrs. Is this why they found the voice for high praise in the suffocating, searing flames of martyrdom?

Jesus is the same yesterday, today, and forever. One day we all will meet him around this dynamic truth. Those of the first century who died for him. Those of the Middle Ages who woke to great themes of Reformation. Those of the twentieth century who linked hands around the globe to evangelize the continents. No matter how the various ages and cultures dressed, no matter their languages, Jesus was and is the same. No wonder the hymnist wrote:

> *People and realms of every tongue*
> *Dwell in his love with sweet accord*

While other nations own their lord
And other worlds attend God's word.
—"Jesus Shall Reign"
Words by Isaac Watts, Music by John Hatton

He is ours—the unforsaking, unchanged Christ—the Lord of our souls!

Questions for Personal Reflection

1. In what ways does our culture attempt to redefine the image of Christ?

2. What is your source for truth when there is confusion about Jesus' constant love for you?

Day 4: My Service to Others
Read Numbers 11:10–15

"I cannot carry all these people by myself; the burden is too heavy for me," lamented Moses (Numbers 11:14). Though God had just saved the nation of Israel, the people, once joyous over their Exodus, now grumbled in their tents. Ministry is delightful when other people thank leaders for their sacrifice, but often, criticism and complaints are more prevalent a response. This grumbling among the body of Christ is a "soul beater" for the spiritual leaders.

How often in a single year does a pastor lament like Moses, "The burden is too heavy for me" (v. 14)? Serving others is a difficult task that is not always appreciated. It takes true faithfulness to persevere. But what Moses failed to realize was that he was not carrying the burden of service all by himself. God was there. God would never give him more than he could handle, but Moses would have to depend on the Lord along the way, in light and heavy times.

As believers we should celebrate the noble men and women who seek to follow the Great Shepherd while they live out their callings to serve. And as we go out to serve as well, we must remember that there is no real antidote for the suffering that, at times, comes along with service but to focus on our responsibilities and trust God. He is faithful, and he strengthens us to continue to serve. We can be sure that as we serve those around us faithfully and in a spirit of love, God will help us carry our burdens.

Questions for Personal Reflection

1. In what ways are you a burden to those who are your spiritual leaders?

2. What are some things you can do to be more supportive of your spiritual

leaders?

Day 5: My Personal Worship

Read Revelation 2:10

"Be faithful, even to the point of death, and I will give you the crown of life," said the angel to the church at Smyrna (Revelation 2:10). The testimonies of martyrs who affirmed this truth continue to amaze and inspire. Consider these philosophies:

Dietrich Bonhoeffer's translation of Luke 9:23 says, "Take up your cross and follow me." Bonhoeffer said that what this really meant was, "Come with me and die."

Think of the martyred missionary Jim Elliot, whose dying philosophy was, "He is no fool who gives what he cannot keep to gain what he cannot lose."

Recall the beloved Reverend Martin Luther King Jr., whose tombstone reads, "Let justice roll down like waters and righteousness like an ever-flowing stream" (Amos 5:24 NASB).

Faithfulness in our spiritual worship calls us all to answer the hymn we so often sing:

> *Must I be carried through the skies*
> *On flowery beds of ease*
> *While others fought to win the prize*
> *And sailed through bloody seas.*
> —"Am I a Soldier of the Cross?"
> Words by Isaac Watts, Music by Thomas Arne

Faithfulness is the currency of martyrs, who spend it down to their very blood.

Questions for Personal Reflection

1. In what ways does your life reflect the faithfulness of the martyrs?

2. How can you become stronger in your commitment to obey God in every aspect of your life?

Day 6: Jeremiah—When the Whole World Disagrees

Read Jeremiah 20:1–12

Israel had two kinds of prophets: false and true. The false ones were always very popular, and the true ones always ... told the truth. Jeremiah was in utter pain because, like preachers in every age, he wanted everyone to just listen to him. But his sermons were so honest and heavy, Jeremiah found himself unwelcome in his own country.

In Jeremiah 20, Pashhur, a well-liked preacher, told Jeremiah to stop preaching such negative sermons. To reinforce his request, he had Jeremiah beaten and put in the stocks at Benjamin Gate, then released the next day. Jeremiah told him, "The LORD's name for you is not Pashhur, but Magor-Missabib" (Jeremiah 20:3). *Pashhur* is Hebrew for "Glad-Free," and *Magor-Missabib* means "Terror on Every Side." So Jeremiah basically said, "Your name is no longer Reverend Glad-Free, it is Dr. Magor-Missabib, Dr. Terror on Every Side" (foreshadowing Pashhur's downfall at the hands of Babylon).

Faithfulness isn't tailoring your sermons for a theological journal. Faithfulness tells the truth even when the truth is not popular. Here was the essence of the sermon Jeremiah preached to one man—Pashhur:

> *I will make you a terror to yourself and to all your friends;*
> *with your own eyes you will see them fall by the sword of*
> *their enemies. I will hand all Judah over to the king of Baby-*

lon, who will carry them away to Babylon or put them to the
sword. I will hand over to their enemies all the wealth of this
city—all its products, all its valuables and all the treasures
of the kings of Judah ... and you Pashhur, and all who live
in your house will go into exile into Babylon. There you will
die and be buried, you and all your friends to whom you
have prophesied lies.
—Jeremiah 20:4–6

It was not the kind of sermon that won friends or put Jeremiah on the career fast-track. But God smiled down on a lone prophet's faithfulness, for God knew Jeremiah would always remain faithful. Jeremiah summed up his own faithfulness this way: "But if I say, 'I will not mention him or speak any more in his name,' his word is in my heart like a fire, a fire shut up in my bones. I am weary of holding it in; indeed, I cannot" (v. 9).

Faithfully and openly praising God's name is the burden of all those who will not trade truth for acceptance. Faithfulness is fire. It scorches the earth with God's requirement even as it consumes the committed.

Questions for Personal Reflection

1. Are you more concerned about being popular or being faithful to God?

2. How do you respond to your ego's attempts to get in the way of your spiritual

commitment?

Day 7: Group Discussion

The following questions should take about forty-five minutes to answer and discuss. Each member should answer the first question, leaving the remaining questions open-ended. Everyone need not answer, but be sure all members participate.

1. *Who in your life most exemplifies faithfulness?*

2. *Faithfulness means God can count on us. In what ways should we be more dependable to God?*

3. *How should our lives reflect the fear of the Lord?*

4. *Jesus is the same yesterday, today, and forever. What is the personal benefit of this truth?*

5. What would be the effect in our lives of our total faithfulness to God—even to the point of death?

6. How do we reconcile the tension between telling the truth of God's Word and our desires to be popular?

Week 4: Faithfulness—Commitment to What Is Right

Memory Passage for the Week: Luke 9:62

Day 1: Faithfulness—Commitment to What Is Right

God has always been faithful to his people, and he always will be faithful. 1 Kings 8:56–61.

Day 2: The Purpose of God in My Life

How did Jeremiah live in a corrupt city? He was faithful to God, and he had a stubborn commitment to what was right. Jeremiah 5:1–2.

Day 3: My Relationship with Christ

Jesus is the source of all healing, and this healing should inspire our true commitment and faithfulness to him. John 9:24–33.

Day 4: My Service to Others

All believers who hold to hate, profit, or prejudice while they pretend devotion are not practicing acceptable faithfulness to God. Nehemiah 5:6–11.

Day 5: My Personal Worship

Daniel's devotion to God could not be threatened out of him, even with death. He praised God no matter what. Daniel 3:17–18.

Day 6: A Character Study on Caleb

Numbers 13:26–14:9

Day 7: Group Discussion

Day 1: Faithfulness—Commitment to What Is Right

Read 1 Kings 8:56–61

When the temple was finished, Solomon blessed Israel for their enduring commitment to obedience. Solomon dedicated the temple by thanking God for three ways he had been faithful, and by asking for four wonderful things for Israel's future. He began with thanksgiving:

1. He was thankful that God gave rest to his people. War was over. Peace had come.
2. He thanked God that he never fell short in a single one of his promises. God kept his word.
3. He thanked God that he was with Israel's fathers between Abram and the present moment.

But Solomon's thanksgiving gives us a reason to believe God will also be faithful in the future. He gave four invocations:

1. He entreated God to remain faithful.
2. He prayed that the hearts of the relatively new nation would turn toward God.
3. He prayed that God would enable Israel to keep all his commandments and live in purity.

4.   Solomon's final request was that God would use Israel's future faithfulness to prove to all the world that Israel's God was the one and only God.

These prayers were said as though Solomon was talking to God while the nation listened—an admirable goal for all national leadership.

Questions for Personal Reflection

1. What are some things for which you are thankful?

2. What are some things you would like God to enable you to do?

Day 2: The Purpose of God in My Life

Read Jeremiah 5:1–2

Jeremiah tested the morality of Jerusalem, exploring the city in hopes of finding honest and upstanding people. But unfortunately, Jerusalem didn't pass the test. All social compassion had been claimed by personal interests and ambitious career goals.

Believers in the closing years of the twentieth century have witnessed the demise of political character. Presidents have faced impeachment trials. The sludge artists of election engineering have forced candidates to resign before and during public elections. Other lawmakers, shamed by public scandal, have resigned before their terms of office were complete. In his day, Jeremiah's jog through Jerusalem found no men and women of character. It leaves me wondering what the prophet would discover if he jogged through the streets of our own nation today.

During a recent political scandal, lawmakers rated perjury, but not adultery, as impeachable. This investigation called into question other lawmakers' character as well. Integrity seemed in short supply. If Jeremiah had ministered in contemporary America, Jeremiah 5:1 might have read, "Go up and down the streets of Washington, look around and consider, search through her squares. If you can find but one person who deals honestly and seeks the truth, I will forgive this city."

God wants us to be a faithful nation. He wants each one of us to fulfill the purposes he has for our lives. When we let bad morals pervade our culture—and we let bad morals pervade our own lives—God's purpose becomes very difficult for us to see, and we have a tendency to become lost.

Questions for Personal Reflection

1. What are some areas of your life in which you need to develop more godly integrity?

2. What excuses do we often give for failing to be people of integrity?

Day 3: My Relationship with Christ

Read John 9:24–33

A man who was born blind refused to sell out for a lie. He had just come into relationship with Christ, inspired by the fact that he just received something he never had before—sight! He could see, and Jesus, his Healer, was the first face he ever saw. Think of the depth of commitment to Christ this must have inspired within the man. Consider the song he might have sung:

I have a gift that makes these
caustic Pharisees seem over-dreary.
I can see the greens and blues of God's
great world better than these men
of God, so long focusing their narrow-
slitted eyes on ink and paper.
It is good to read his word and the
Pharisees can do it well.
But who would read of God when they
might have him in for dinner.
This is the sin of learned men: they study
in the dim light of sooty rooms,
While God is circling with the white
gulls against the blue-fire dawn of sky.

How poor are they who cannot look up
from dull dogma and see that
God is seated at the very table where they sit.

Questions for Personal Reflection

1. What "song" does your life sing in response to all God has done for you?

2. How can your song affect the lives of people who do not know Jesus Christ?

Day 4: My Service to Others

Read Nehemiah 5:6–11

How do the redeemed treat the redeemed? Faithfulness is a commitment to what's right in the way we treat our brothers and sisters.

Someone I know once said he would be a Christian if it weren't for Christians. I wonder if he had witnessed those who claim the name of Christ mistreating each other.

There is a story that circulated among one of the high reformed churches of South Africa during the terrible days of apartheid. In those days (similar to America's civil rights struggle) blacks were not permitted to worship or pray in white churches. Blacks who tried to crash these "color lines" were thrown out of the church by the angry whites who worshiped there.

On one occasion a very wealthy white woman knelt to pray on the kneeler of her church pew, and noticed a black woman down on her knees just ahead of her. "What are you doing in this church?" shouted the angry white woman.

"Nothin' ma'am, just scrubbing the floor—I'm the new janitor. The church hired me just this morning."

"Oh, alright," said the white woman, softening her insulting tone. "But God help you if I catch you praying."

When Christians mistreat each other, Christ bleeds yet again. Nehemiah would chastise all believers who hold to hate, profit, or prejudice while they pretend devotion.

Questions for Personal Reflection

1. Have you ever been mistreated by someone claiming to be a believer? If so, what was the effect of that mistreatment on your life?

2. How can we guard against mistreating fellow believers?

Day 5: My Personal Worship

Read Daniel 3:17—18

God can deliver us from every trial—yet he doesn't. As Daniel squared off against Darius, maybe he realized he was among the few Israelites who survived the Babylonian siege and subsequent horror of Persian captivity. He knew many who had died; he had heard the old ones tell of the three-year siege where the starving Jews resorted to cannibalism.

Why then would he have believed that God was more prone to rescue him than the thousands who paid in blood before Nebuchadnezzar burned and leveled the city? The truth is, he didn't know. He was upfront with the Persian king. God was able to deliver him from the lions' den. In fact, God could have crushed Darius like a fly on a tile wall. But even if he didn't save Daniel—as he had not done for thousands before him—one thing was still not for sale: Daniel's determination to worship the true God even in a pagan culture.

Daniel might have had to die, but he didn't have to be unfaithful.

God would be God, celebrated by Daniel's life or Daniel's death.

So fill the lions' den, starve the lions, and throw commitment to the beasts. There will be no compromise. It is as easy for the committed to worship in the company of beasts as in the temple.

Questions for Personal Reflection

1. What are those challenges that tempt you to compromise your faith?

2. How might you have responded had you been in Daniel's situation?

Day 6: Caleb—God Plus One Equals a Majority

Read Numbers 13:26–14:9

The dreams of God always require faithfulness. His tasks are usually difficult, requiring time and energy to get the job done.

So it was with the conquest of Canaan. For generations God told Israel he would give them Canaan, a land flowing with milk and honey. It sounded good until they went to pick up the gift and discovered people were already living in Canaan. So the gift required a great deal of effort from Israel. It is in this same sense that God gives us eternal life, only to have us discover that we must work out our own salvation (Philippians 2:12) and faithfully discipline ourselves to make our lives really count for God.

So the spies returned with a majority and a minority report. The majority (ten of them) said, "We went into the land to which you sent us, and it does flow with milk and honey! Here is its fruit. But the people who live there are powerful, and the cities are fortified and very large. We even saw descendants of Anak there" (Numbers 13:27–28). So, after they rehearsed the size and strength of the cities, they pointed out to Moses that God's gift was already owned by other people: "The Amalekites live in the Negev; the Hittites, Jebusites and Amorites live in the hill country; and the Canaanites live near the sea and along the Jordan" (v. 29).

But worst of all was the size of the inhabitants. These were big people, said the majority of the spies: "We can't attack those people; they are stronger than we are.... We seemed like grasshoppers in our own eyes, and we looked the same to them" (vv. 31,33).

Enter the minority report: the faithful Caleb and Joshua.

Caleb knew that with God all things are possible, and that God and any size army form a powerful majority. So while the people began to moan, "If only we had died in Egypt" (Numbers 14:2)—a mystique that lacked motivational force—Joshua had a word of faith: "The land we passed through and explored is exceedingly good. If the LORD is pleased with us, he will lead us in that land.... Only do not rebel against the LORD" (vv. 7–9).

Faithfulness is the only response real believers make to the will of God. Caleb and Joshua lived long enough to dwell in that good land. Faithfulness was the key to their triumph.

Faithfulness is the energy that keeps on keeping on.

Faithfulness sees giants and doesn't compare them to itself. It sets giants next to God and wonders why anyone would ever be afraid.

Faithfulness desires a clear word, not an easy word.

Faithfulness pities those who think numbers alone constitute strength.

Faithfulness knows that God plus one is a clear majority.

Questions for Personal Reflection

1. What big task(s) has God placed before you?

2. In evaluating God's call in your life, are you yielding to the majority report

(I can't do this!) or to the minority report (God will make a way!)? Explain your

response.

Day 7: Group Discussion

The following questions should take about forty-five minutes to answer and discuss. Each member should answer the first question, leaving the remaining questions open-ended. Everyone need not answer, but be sure all members participate.

1. *In what ways has God revealed his faithfulness in your life?*

2. *What are some things we can do to develop God's character in our lives?*

3. *How can God's work in and through our lives encourage others we know?*

4. *How should believers treat each other? What are the results of failing to do this?*

5. How can we guard against the pressure to abandon the faith in favor of a watered-down religion?

6. How does a steadfast commitment to God serve as motivation to persevere in doing what is right?

Week 5: Faithfulness—No Compromise

Memory Passage for the Week: Esther 4:16

Day 1: Faithfulness—No Compromise

Faithfulness is a refusal to betray any truth in our central value system. Jeremiah 20:9.

Day 2: The Purpose of God in My Life

Stephen, a martyr, died an example that the purpose to which God calls us is not always easy to carry out. Acts 7:54–60.

Day 3: My Relationship with Christ

Our steadfast defense of Christ will evoke his steadfast defense of our lives. Matthew 10:17–20.

Day 4: My Service to Others

Regardless of whatever opposition we face, God's armor protects us, and we can faithfully move forward to achieve his Great Commission. Ephesians 6:10–18.

Day 5: My Personal Worship

Jeremiah exulted with that wonderful assurance that so often marks our worship: those who love God are never cast away; God's love is unfailing. Lamentations 3:31–33.

Day 6: The Final Judgment

Matthew 25:31–46

Day 7: Group Discussion

Day 1: Faithfulness—No Compromise

Read Jeremiah 20:9

Faithfulness is a fire in the bones. It may falter in moments of weakness, but it will not stop burning. Faithfulness is a refusal to betray any truth in our central value system. Faithfulness does not compromise.

The Cross is the best example of facing extremes without any sense of compromise. Jesus was the no-quit Christ who demonstrated how to hold to principle, even to the point of death. Years ago I wrote in my book *Once Upon a Tree*:

> *Joseph Wittig once said, "A man's biography ought really to begin not with his birth but with his death; it can be written only from the point of view of its end, because only from there can the whole of his life in its fulfillment be seen." So it is that when we tell anyone of Jesus we must begin with his death. One cannot even begin to understand the life of Christ without understanding his death. It is here at the cross that his biography begins.* [4]

"Self-sacrifice" is another way to say "self-denial." Jeremiah denied himself in favor of what God wanted. There at Benjamin Gate, things were far from pleasant—but Jeremiah realized his faithfulness had brought about his suffering. Times were hard. The city would soon fall, and Jeremiah understood that the small coins of self-denial were required to buy the great commitments of life. Anticipating our dying times reminds us that life is inherently serious. The apostle Paul said that he was "being poured out like a drink offering" (Philippians 2:17). Indeed, all human life is being poured out, either in self-concern or in service. Jeremiah's life was being poured out in utter faithfulness and no compromise.

Questions for Personal Reflection

1. Are you sacrificing things in your life so that you can experience the life God has in store for you?

2. What are some ways that you can be more sacrificial in your life?

Day 2: The Purpose of God in My Life
Acts 7:54–60

The writers of the New Testament documented Jesus' final words on the cross: "My God, my God, why have you forsaken me?" (Mark 15:34); "I am thirsty" (John 19:28); "Father, into your hands I commit my spirit" (Luke 23:46); and so on. These cries are what we refer to as "The Seven Last Words of Jesus." These final words invite us to also consider what we could call "The Four Last Sentences of Stephen" in the book of Acts:

Sentence #1: "Which of the prophets did your fathers not persecute? ... They killed those who foretold the coming of the Just One, of whom you now have become the betrayers and murderers, who have received the law by the direction of angels and have not kept it" (Acts 7:52–53 NKJV).
This blatant honesty was bound to get Stephen in trouble, but faithfulness means that you don't tell the truth only when it's convenient. Stephen told all the truth all the time. This was his definition of faithfulness.

Sentence #2: "Look! I see the heavens opened and the Son of Man standing at the right hand of God!" (v. 56 NKJV).
Being faithful is always rewarded by a vision of God. Too great a claim? Not at all, for either in life (as in Stephen's case during the last moments of his life) or in death, we shall wake to some vision of triumph.

Sentence #3: "Lord Jesus, receive my spirit" (v. 59 NKJV).

Stephen, bleeding among the flying stones, confessed his final confidence. The faithful are familiar with the confidence to greet our eternal Christ without fear.

Sentence #4: "Lord, do not charge them with this sin" (v. 60 NKJV).

Faithful men and women are never vindictive, even during their executions. Stephen modeled his last words after some of Jesus' last words. Jesus was faithful in carrying out his Father's will without being vindictive. Stephen, desiring to be like Jesus, could hardly do less.

Questions for Personal Reflection

1. How can you develop the depth of commitment demonstrated by Stephen?

2. How does the world respond to the steadfast commitment of godly people?

Day 3: My Relationship with Christ

Read Matthew 10:17–20

Jesus will supply to us in our time of need exactly what we need to sustain us. Can we trust his faithfulness? Of course we can. Jesus himself is the source of our faithfulness. Dr. James A. Harnish asked the question, "Where do we find the power to be a disciple?":

> *Where do we find the power to keep going when the going*
> *really gets tough? Where do we find the power to continue to*
> *believe in love in a world that is filled with hate? ... Where*
> *do we find the power to continue to believe in good in a world*
> *that is filled with so much evil?*[5]

The answer is Jesus, who supplies the recipe for our relationship with him. He stands by us, supplying us the power to stand for him. Once again, where do we find that living water, where we are refreshed by his faithfulness? All these things are found in our faithfulness—there or nowhere!

Questions for Personal Reflection

1. What are some of the things you may have substituted for an authentic relationship with God?

2. What are your sources of spiritual power, and how often do you tap into those sources?

Day 4: My Service to Others

Read Ephesians 6:10–18

Paul told the Ephesians to take a stand, and the same applies to us. But take a stand against what, or rather, against whom? Jesus taught us to pray, "Deliver us from the evil one" (Matthew 6:13). The evil one is the ever-present, ever-challenging force that daily comes against our faithfulness. You may be sure that if Satan had his way, our resolve to stand true would crumble. So Paul said we have to dress for the onslaught. We have to wear the armor, clothing ourselves for the fray.

You will notice that of all the panoply of armor, only in Ephesians 6:17 do we come across the single piece of armor that is offensive in nature—the sword of the Spirit. All the other pieces are defensive. With the faithful protection of God's armor, we are ready to defeat Satan in battle. He is called by many names:

Abaddon, the Destroyer, Revelation 9:11

The Accuser, Revelation 12:10

The Adversary, 1 Peter 5:8 (NKJV)

The Murderer, John 8:44

The Evil One, Matthew 13:19

But regardless of his opposition, God's armor protects us, and we can advance faithfully, moving forward to achieve God's Great Commission with the sword of the Spirit.

Questions for Personal Reflection

1. What has been the end result of letting down your spiritual guard?

2. Why is it so important to defend ourselves against Satan's attacks?

Day 5: My Personal Worship

Read Lamentations 3:31–33

"No compromise" faithfulness is hardly said better than in Lamentations 3:31–33. Consider the fourfold promise of these verses to all who believe.

Promise #1: "For men are not cast off by the Lord forever" (v. 31). We should rejoice daily that God is in the business of saving us forever—no true believer is ever cast off.

Promise #2: "Though he brings grief, he will show compassion" (v. 32). God, like a loving parent, cannot stand to see his children cry. He consoles his weeping children.

Promise #3: "So great is his unfailing love" (v. 32). His love surpasses all the rapids and waterfalls on this earth—it has never ceased to flow.

Promise #4: "He does not willingly bring affliction or grief to the children of men" (v.33). When you cry, God, too, is broken.

God is so good, and his faithfulness is worthy of our praise. Indeed when we are faithful, his faithfulness constantly supplies protection, and his blessing and love arrive with each new sunrise. His faithfulness is worthy of our faithful praise.

Questions for Personal Reflection

1. How have you benefited from those times when you have trusted God's love?

2. How does your own love for him affect your attitude toward each new day?

Day 6: The Final Judgment

MATTHEW 25:31–46 (TLB)

But when I, the Messiah, shall come in my glory, and all the angels with me, then I shall sit upon my throne of glory. And all the nations shall be gathered before me. And I will separate the people as a shepherd separates the sheep from the goats, and place the sheep at my right hand, and the goats at my left.

Then I, the King, shall say to those at my right, "Come, blessed of my Father, into the Kingdom prepared for you from the founding of the world. For I was hungry and you fed me; I was thirsty and you gave me water; I was a stranger and you invited me into your homes; naked and you clothed me; sick and in prison, and you visited me."

Then these righteous ones will reply, "Sir, when did we ever see you hungry and feed you? Or thirsty and give you anything to drink? Or a stranger, and help you? Or naked, and clothe you? When did we ever see you sick or in prison, and visit you?"

And I, the King, will tell them, "When you did it to these my brothers you were doing it to me!" Then I will turn to those on my left and say, "Away with you, you cursed ones, into the eternal fire prepared for the devil and his demons. For I was hungry and you wouldn't feed me; thirsty, and you wouldn't give me anything to drink; a stranger, and you refused me hospitality; naked, and you wouldn't clothe me; sick, and in prison, and you didn't visit me."

Then they will reply, "Lord, when did we ever see you hungry or thirsty or a stranger or naked or sick or in prison, and not help you?"

And I will answer, "When you refused to help the least of these my brothers, you were refusing to help me."

And they shall go away into eternal punishment; but the righteous into everlasting life.

Questions for Personal Reflection

1. Jesus distinguished between the righteous and the unrighteous. Which category are you in, and how do you know?

2. What do you imagine everlasting life in Christ to be like?

Day 7: Group Discussion

The following questions should take about forty-five minutes to answer and discuss. Each member should answer the first question, leaving the remaining questions open-ended. Everyone need not answer, but be sure all members participate.

1. *Do you consider yourself to be an optimist or a pessimist? What do you think your optimistic/pessimistic attitude says about your faithfulness?*

2. *Stephen spoke with truth and suffered the earthly consequences. What are the earthly consequences of speaking God's truth today?*

3.   *How can we keep from betraying God's truth and his value system?*

4.   *How can we find the power to be disciples of Jesus?*

5. *How should we respond when we are tempted?*

6. *What is the source of your future hope? How does it affect your interactions with unbelievers?*

Week 6: Faithfulness—The Road That Ends in Victory

Memory Passage for the Week: Deuteronomy 7:9

Day 1: Faithfulness—The Road That Ends in Victory

Faithfulness always ends in victory. The second coming of Christ will be a powerful celebration—only the faithful will be celebrated. Revelation 19:11–16.

Day 2: The Purpose of God in My Life

Nothing is able to separate us from God's love. All we are required to do is to remain faithful—no matter what trials we face. Romans 8:37–39.

Day 3: My Relationship with Christ

To all who overcome the trials of their faith, Jesus promises to give the right to rule with him on his throne. Revelation 3:20–21.

Day 4: My Service to Others

Jesus condemned the rich man not because he was rich, but because his wealth blinded him to the needs of those around him. Luke 16:19–25.

Day 5: My Personal Worship

Faithfulness in personal worship is a jewel in the soul of the believer. Hebrews 10:25.

Day 6: Verses for Further Reflection

Day 7: Group Discussion

Day 1: Faithfulness—The Road That Ends in Victory
Read Revelation 19:11–16

The final triumph of the apocalypse is the appearance of the white rider. Across his chest and on his thigh is a name—King of kings and Lord of lords.

The white rider is Jesus, but he, in this account, is called Faithful and True. Jesus, God's Son, patiently endured the Cross so that he might finish the task that his Father gave him to complete. If there is any doubt that faithfulness is the road that leads to victory, we have Revelation 2:10 for confirmation: "Be faithful, even to the point of death, and I will give you the crown of life."

Faithfulness always ends in victory. How complete is this victory? These are the ten facets of victory in Revelation 21:

- The dwelling of God will be with humankind (v. 3).
- God will wipe away all tears (v. 4).
- There will be no more death (v. 4).
- There will be no more pain (v. 4).
- Everything will be made new (v. 5).
- Anyone thirsty may drink from the spring of the water of life (v. 6).
- We will be in the presence of the celestial wedding party (v. 9).
- We will live in a jewel-encrusted new city (vv. 15–21).

🐦 Nothing impure will enter the city (v. 27).

🐦 All our neighbors will be those whose names are written in the Lamb's book of life (v. 27).

All in all, the Second Coming is a celebration of the faithful. All they have endured now ends in victory. Revelation 19:6 reminds us that the faithful will sing with innumerable hosts: "Hallelujah! For our Lord God Almighty reigns."

Questions for Personal Reflection

1. What emotions come to mind as you consider the future return of Christ?

2. How can this reality serve as motivation to share God's love with as many people as possible?

Day 2: The Purpose of God in My Life

Read Romans 8:37–39

I once traveled in India, near the Pakistan border. There I met a Christian who once was not only a Muslim but a member of the Russian army and a tank commando during the war in Afghanistan. When he accepted Christ, he became an outcast and a renegade to his Islamic family. When we met, he was on the run in Northwest India. I asked him if he had any regrets about the price he had to pay to know Christ.

He grinned broadly. "Christ," he said, "paid so great a price for me, my own poor sufferings amount to nothing."

He caused me to remember what Paul said: "I consider that our present sufferings are not worth comparing with the glory that will be revealed in us" (Romans 8:18).

This young Christian proved daily that faithfulness always brings victory. This passage in Romans makes it clear that nothing can ever separate us from the love of God.

Paul specifically named ten things that cannot separate us from the love of God. Read the verses and add them up. Could these keep us from enjoying the benefits of his love?

> *No, in all these things we are more than conquerors through him who loved us. For I am convinced that neither death nor life, neither angels nor demons, neither the present nor the fu-*

ture, nor any powers, neither height nor depth, nor anything else in all creation, will be able to separate us from the love of God that is in Christ Jesus our Lord.
—Romans 8:37–39

Questions for Personal Reflection

1. What are the daily benefits of Christ's suffering on your behalf?

2. What should be your response to the realization that Christ died for you?

Day 3: My Relationship with Christ

Read Revelation 3:20–21

This was Christ's promise to the Laodicean church in Revelation 3:21: "To him who overcomes, I will give the right to sit with me on my throne." We are destined for the throne. But a few things are in order before we achieve this destiny.

Overcoming first! Reigning next! Faithfulness, then triumph! This was the Laodicean progression.

The Laodicean church was powerful and wealthy. But power and wealth bred complacency and an awful reluctance to practice self-denial. While they lived this complacent life, others suffered and died under intense waves of persecution. In verse 20, Jesus reminded the Laodiceans that he stood at the door of history and was about to reenter time for the grand reckoning. He urged them to resist compromise so they could triumph.

In a popular parable, when Jesus reentered heaven after his resurrection, God asked him, "Son, have you redeemed the world I sent you forth to save?"

"I have," said the Son.

"Son," said the Father, "were you successful in redeeming the world?"

"Some were saved," replied the Son.

"Some?" asked the Father.

"Twelve or so," said the Son.

"What, no more? Have you any evidence that your mission was a serious struggle to redeem?"

At this the Son held out his hands. "These," he said, "I gained in loving earth. I have no other evidence but these."

The Father gazed upon his hands and wept. The Father's tears were molten gold and as they fell, they collected into a circlet of bright light. Then he took the crown fashioned from his tears and set it on the Savior's head.

All heaven stood in silence before this simple truth: tears are the stuff of which all crowns are made.

Questions for Personal Reflection

1. If faithfulness is required in order to triumph, what do you need to do to be sure you will be triumphant?

2. What does it mean that "tears are the stuff of which all crowns are made"?

Day 4: My Service to Others
Read Luke 16:19–25

The Pharisees believed that wealthy people became rich because of their obedience to God. But in this passage a rich man went to hell, not for being wealthy, but for refusing to care about those less fortunate.

Hell is haunted! There ran through all its fiery halls the specter of a man who once was rich. He wailed from year to year, "Send Lazarus to dip the tip of his finger in water and cool my tongue, because I am in agony in this fire" (Luke 16:24).

The cry was constant and eternal: "SEND LAZARUS, send Lazarus ... send Lazarus ... for I am tormented in this flame."

But who was Lazarus? A man for whom life had gone hard. He once lived and begged at the rich man's gate. When the world was generous, he ate. When the world was stingy, he starved. Hunger wasn't his passport into heaven. He went to heaven because, whether hungry or full, he was faithful.

Those who so often go without in this world must be surprised at the level of their inheritance the moment they enter heaven. There is a popular tale of two retiring missionaries, who spent their lives serving Christ. It is said that they returned to America on the same ship with Teddy Roosevelt, who was returning from an African hunting safari. When the ship docked in New York, bands played and crowds amassed to greet the returning president. The old missionary turned to his wife and said, "See!

From a single hunting trip, the president returns to ticker tape parades and marching bands; but when we come home there's no one here to meet us."

"My dear," said his wife with a broad grin, "we're not home yet."

Lazarus must have had a welcome in heaven that would make a returning president feel anonymous. Faithfulness is the road that always ends in victory.

Questions for Personal Reflection

1. Are you living for a reward in this life or in the next? Explain your response.

2. How can you resist the urge to seek worldly accolades while serving God?

Day 5: My Personal Worship
Read Hebrews 10:25

The church: it's always there. Sometimes interesting, many times not, but it's always there. There's virtue in attending church, for there we meet with God and those who love him. Why is this one-hour meeting time so special? Here are ten reasons to go to church:

10. There is one place that constantly reminds us that heaven exists—it's the church.

9. God's house is a constant reminder to the nation that it ought to be more like God's house.

8. God's house is a place of worship, and worship is a hassle-stopper. Those who constantly run without stopping for God eventually become all legs and no heart.

7. Church is a routine of re-energizing. Most of our routines make for weariness, but church makes for vitality.

6. Church teaches our children the life of faith. It trains our children to become tomorrow's moral giants.

5. There we live in a community of need—our brothers and sisters, like ourselves, have many needs. We can lift them up as they lift us.

4. The church is a place of praise, and praise keeps us from losing hope in a world overrun with despair.

3. The Bible is read in church. Just to hear these ancient words of God gives us the power to triumph over momentary problems.

2. The gospel is preached there, and where the gospel is preached people come to Christ.

1. Jesus is exalted there, and anywhere that Christ is exalted is a place where our spirits soar.

Hebrews 10:25 is a call not just to worship, but to worship in a specific place, where altars are central and God is expected to show up.

Questions for Personal Reflection

1. When it comes to worship, are you a spectator or a participant?

2. What are some ways in which your life is strengthened by your worship?

Day 6: Verses for Further Reflection

John 8:31: To the Jews who had believed him, Jesus said, "If you hold to my teaching, you are really my disciples."

John 8:51: I tell you the truth, if anyone keeps my word, he will never see death.

John 15:10: If you obey my commands, you will remain in my love, just as I have obeyed my Father's commands and remain in his love.

1 Corinthians 1:9: God, who has called you into fellowship with his son Jesus Christ our Lord, is faithful.

1 Corinthians 10:13: No temptation has seized you except what is common to man. And God is faithful; he will not let you be tempted beyond what you can bear. But when you are tempted, he will also provide a way out so that you can stand up under it.

1 Thessalonians 5:24: The one who calls you is faithful and he will do it.

2 Thessalonians 3:3: But the Lord is faithful, and he will strengthen and protect you from the evil one.

Hebrews 3:6: But Christ is faithful as a son over God's house. And we are his house, if we hold on to our courage and the hope of which we boast.

ACTS 26:1–6, 12–20

Then Agrippa said to Paul, "You have permission to speak for yourself." So Paul motioned with his hand and began his defense: "King Agrippa, I consider myself fortunate to stand before you today as I make my defense against all the accusations of the Jews, and especially so because you are well acquainted with all the Jewish customs and controversies. Therefore, I beg you to listen to me patiently.

"The Jews all know the way I have lived ever since I was a child, from the beginning of my life in my own country, and also in Jerusalem. They have known me for a long time and can testify, if they are willing, that according to the strictest sect of our religion, I lived as a Pharisee. And now it is because of my hope in what God has promised our fathers that I am on trial today....

"On one of these journeys I was going to Damascus with the authority and commission of the chief priests. About noon, O king, as I was on the road, I saw a light from heaven, brighter than the sun, blazing around me and my companions. We all fell to the ground, and I heard a voice saying to me in Aramaic, 'Saul, Saul, why do your persecute me? It is hard for you to kick against the goads.'

"Then I asked, 'Who are you, Lord?'

"'I am Jesus, whom you are persecuting,' the Lord replied. 'Now get up and stand on your feet. I have appeared to you to appoint you as a servant and as a witness of what you have seen of me and what I will show you. I will rescue you from your own people and from the Gentiles. I am sending you to them to open their eyes and turn them from darkness to light, and from the power of Satan to God, so that they may receive forgiveness of sins and a place among those who are sanctified by faith in me.'

"So then, King Agrippa, I was not disobedient to the vision from heaven. First to those in Damascus, then to those in Jerusalem and in all Judea, and to the Gentiles also, I preached that they should repent and turn to God and prove their repentance by their deeds."

Questions for Personal Reflection

1. What does your own encounter with the faithfulness of Christ lead you to do?

2. How can God use you to reach other people?

Day 7: Group Discussion

The following questions should take about forty-five minutes to answer and discuss. Each member should answer the first question, leaving the remaining questions open-ended. Everyone need not answer, but be sure all members participate.

1. *Would you agree that complacency is prevalent in today's culture? What are some examples?*

2. *How do our present sufferings compare to the sufferings of Jesus Christ?*

3. *What does Christ's return mean in terms of the way we should live our lives today?*

4. *The story of the rich man and Lazarus teaches us something about priorities. How can we prevent our priorities from being overwhelmed by worldliness?*

5. *What is the role of worship in your spiritual life?*

6. *As we reflect on our faithfulness to God and his faithfulness to us, what should be our prayers to him?*

ENDNOTES

1. *Gene Edwards,* A Tale of Three Kings *(Auburn, ME: Christian Books, 1980)* 13.

2. *Thomas À Kempis,* The Imitation of Christ *(Milwaukee: Bruce Publishing, 1949).*

3. *Frederick Faber,* The Fear of God: The Christian Book of Mystical Verse, *Ed: A.W. Tozer (Harrisburg, PA: Christian Publications, 1963)* 18–20.

4. *Calvin Miller,* The Book of Jesus *(NY: Simon & Schuster, 1996)* 445–46.

5. *James A. Harnish, as quoted by Leonard Sweet in* A Cup of Coffee at the Soul Café *(Nashville, TN: Broadman & Holman, 1998)* 50.